Cool
SCHOOL
VOLUNTEERING

Karen Latchana Kenney

A Division of ABDO
ABDO
Publishing Company

visit us at www.abdopublishing.com

Published by ABDO Publishing Company, a division of ABDO, P.O. Box 398166, Minneapolis, Minnesota 55439. Copyright © 2011 by Abdo Consulting Group, Inc. International copyrights reserved in all countries. No part of this book may be reproduced in any form without written permission from the publisher. Checkerboard Library™ is a trademark and logo of ABDO Publishing Company.

Printed in the United States of America, North Mankato, Minnesota
112010
012011

 PRINTED ON RECYCLED PAPER

Editor: Liz Salzmann
Series Concept: Nancy Tuminelly
Cover and Interior Design: Anders Hanson, Mighty Media, Inc.
Photo Credits: Anders Hanson, Shutterstock, Thinkstock

The following manufacturers/names appearing in this book are trademarks:
Aleen's® Tacky Glue®, Elmer's® Glue-All™, Fiskars®, Tulip® Crystals®

Library of Congress Cataloging-in-Publication Data

Kenney, Karen Latchana.
  Cool school volunteering : fun ideas and activities to build school spirit / Karen Latchana Kenney.
    p. cm.
  Includes index.
  ISBN 978-1-61714-670-1
  1. Service learning--Juvenile literature. 2. Voluntarism--Juvenile literature. 3. Young volunteers in social service--Juvenile literature. I. Title.
  LC220.5.K465 2011
  361.3'7--dc22
                    2010024869

Contents

What's Cool About Volunteering?

Going to school is not just about homework and tests. You get to meet new friends and learn amazing new things. Plus, there are so many activities to do and fun groups to join.

Being excited about school is your school spirit. One way to show it is by joining a school group. What do you love doing? Can you dance or sing? Or, do you like to play games or learn languages? Guess what?

School groups are filled with other students who like doing the same things as you!

Volunteer groups are really cool to join! Do you like to help others? That's what volunteers do. They work together to do good things for the community. If you want to show school spirit, a volunteer group may be the right group for you!

Before You Start

It's a good idea to do some research before joining a group. Talk to the members and ask questions. Go to a few meetings and volunteer events. See if the group is one you *want* to join and *can* join.

Time

> How often does the group meet?

> How long are meetings?

> Are there any trips required?

Skills

> What do members do at volunteer sites?

> Do I need special skills to volunteer?

> How do I join the group?

Cost

> Do I need to pay a group fee?

> Are there costs for trips or outings?

Permission

Once you've done your research, check it out with your parents. Make sure you get permission to join the group. You may need a parent's help to fill out an **application** or registration form.

The World of Volunteering

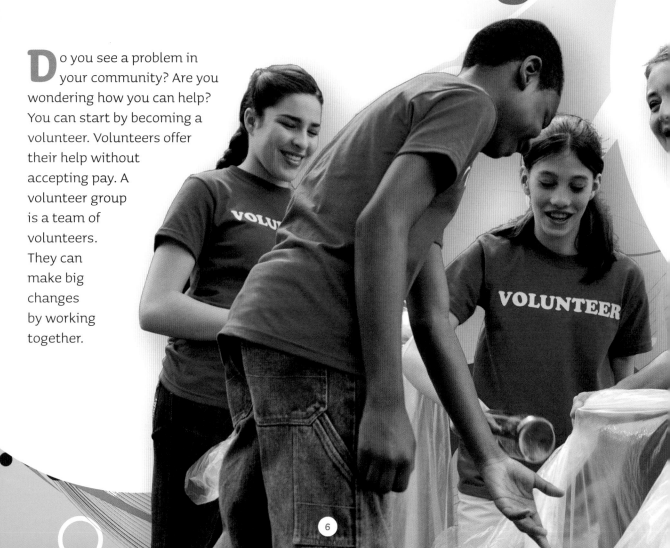

Do you see a problem in your community? Are you wondering how you can help? You can start by becoming a volunteer. Volunteers offer their help without accepting pay. A volunteer group is a team of volunteers. They can make big changes by working together.

A volunteer group can work for one cause or many. A cause is something that needs or deserves help. There are global and local causes that need volunteers. Pick a cause that you care about. Then see how your group can make a difference.

What do volunteers get out of it? Much more than you can imagine! Volunteers learn about other people and different **cultures**. They develop new skills and talents. Trying new things gives people a new **perspective** on life. Plus, working in a team is fun. Teammates make great friends!

What will you learn from volunteering? Join a volunteer group and find out. You'll soon see the difference you can make in the world.

Way Back

The American Red Cross helps victims of **disasters**. Clara Barton started the American Red Cross in 1881. Its first cause was a forest fire in Michigan that year. The fire left thousands of people without homes, food, and jobs. The Red Cross collected **donations** of food, clothing, household items, and money. They delivered these things to the people in need. Today, 96 percent of the people working for the Red Cross are volunteers.

Tools & Supplies

Here are some of the materials you'll need to make the projects in this book!

paper

colored paper

magazines

fabric paint

scrapbooking paper

blank cards with envelopes

fabric scraps

pen

pencil

markers

cotton sweatshirt

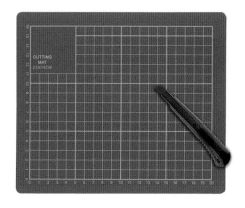

craft knife and cutting mat

scissors

scrapbooking
scissors

cookie cutters

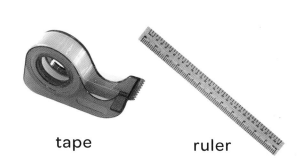

tape

ruler

glue

ribbon

We Need You to Volunteer!

How can you help those in need? Join a volunteer group and get **involved**. It will change your life and the lives of others. You can do great things for your community!

FOOD DRIVE

When you volunteer, you are helping your community and the world. There are different issues your group can focus on. Hunger and homelessness affect many people. Animals are abandoned or mistreated. Find an issue that you care about. Then discover the ways you can volunteer to help.

To help in a big way, you need a lot of people in your group! Get new members by talking with people. **Describe** the cool ways you help. Talk about how volunteering makes you feel and what you learn. Hand out flyers and make posters. Tell students about meetings and activities. Soon, you will have new members who are excited to volunteer!

Come Change Lives With Us!

Hand out flyers and watch your group grow.

What You'll Need

paper, pencil, magazines, scissors, tape or glue, markers, photocopier

1 Decide what kind of message you want on your flyer. Where do you volunteer? Who do you help? Make a list of ideas. Vote on the best ideas to use.

2 Now, look for pictures in magazines to cut out. Choose pictures related to your group's cause.

3 Sketch your flyer in pencil. Put a title at the top. You could say, "Join the Volunteer Club!" or, "Come Change Lives With Us!"

4 Below the title, **describe** where you volunteer and what you do. Try, "**Senior** Home—We sing songs for seniors!" Or, "Animal Shelter—We help groom animals!"

5 At the bottom, write when and where the volunteer group meets. Invite students to come to the next meeting.

6 Tape or glue the pictures around the border of the flyer. Then trace over the pencil with markers. Use color to make it stand out!

7 Make copies on a photocopier and hand out your new flyers!

Let's Help Together!

Volunteering is all about people power! It takes a team to accomplish big things. Good teamwork also makes the work more fun. What can your group achieve as a team?

14

What's Your Thing?

Use this survey to find the best way for group members to volunteer!

Name: _____

What's Your Thing?

Personality
Leader
Planner
Easy going
Worrier
Independent
Energetic
Follower
Patient

Likes
Reading
Outdoors
Internet
Music
Animals
People
Food
Crafts

Talents
Musical
Hardworking
Problem-Solver
Good Listener
Good Reader
Athletic
Cooking
Artistic

Places
Schools
Animal Shelters
Senior Homes
Library
Soup Kitchen
Hospitals
Community Center
Parks/Outdoors

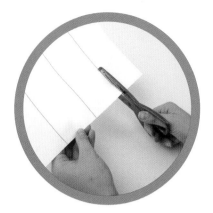

1 Cut four pieces of paper about 2½ x 6½ inches (6.5 x 16.5 cm). Use scrapbooking scissors to give them fun edges.

2 Write a heading at the top of each piece of paper. Use headings such as "Personality," "Likes," "Talents," and "Places." Under each heading, list different options that relate to the heading. See page 15 for ideas.

3 Cut a strip of paper that is about ½ x 2¼ inches (1.3 x 5.7 cm). Try using colored paper. Write "Name" and a blank line on it.

4 Cut a strip of colored paper for the title of your survey. It should be about 1 x 6 inches (2.5 x 15.2 cm). Write the title on it.

5

Arrange the parts of the survey on a piece of colored paper. When they are the way you want them, glue them down.

6

Make copies of the survey. Give one to each member of your group.

7

Have group members write their names on their surveys. Then they should read the words under "Personality," "Likes," and "Talents." Have them circle the ones that **describe** them best. Then they should circle the options under "places" where they would like to volunteer.

8

Collect the surveys. Divide the group by the places they want to volunteer. Give the surveys back to the members. Have them pass them around and get to know the other members. Now they can talk about the best ways to help out in the community!

Be Seen in the Community!

When you are out in the community, let people know who you are. Show your group's logo on T-shirts or flyers. People will know that your group cares!

Groups use logos to show their group identity. A logo is something that can be used on posters, banners, and other printed pieces. It is a symbol that represents a group. Logos can have pictures and words, and the colors are important too.

The following activity will help you create a logo for your volunteer group. Be creative and make it look great. Then use it in different ways to represent your group!

Organized by the Super Tutors

Use your logo to let people know who you are!

What You'll Need

pencil, paper, markers

1 Start with a **brainstorming session** with your group. Ask questions such as *Should our logo have a theme? What words or letters should be in our logo? What picture should be in our logo? What colors should be in our logo?* Write the ideas down.

2 Go through the list with the group. Vote for the best idea for each question and circle it.

3 Now sketch out your idea. Decide what shape you want your logo to fit inside. It could be a triangle or diamond shape. Draw your shape on a piece of paper.

4 Put the picture and words inside the shape. You might need to make several sketches. Move the picture and words around. See what works best. Remember to keep it simple!

5 Show the sketches to your group. What do the other members think? Pick out the logo that everyone likes.

6 Now make a final sketch on a new piece of paper. Make the lines clear and sharp. This will help it look good whether it's printed big or small.

7 Color your logo with markers. Use only a few colors. The colors should look clean and bright.

Help Us Help Others!

DONATE

One way to help others is by raising money. Have a **fund-raiser**. It's fun! Then **donate** the money or buy supplies for people in need.

The first step in fund-raising is setting goals. What are you trying to achieve? Do you need to buy books for kids? Or do you want to make a donation to a food shelf? Set your goal and then figure out how much money you need.

How are you going to raise funds? There are many things you can do. You can have a bake sale or a craft sale. Or you could hold a walk-a-thon.

Brainstorm ideas with the group. There may be costs to put on your fund-raiser. Include the amount you spend when deciding how much money you need.

At your fund-raiser, be friendly and show appreciation. Let people know how their money will help people in need. They will feel good knowing they helped the community!

Do's and Don'ts

Do

- Listen to everyone's brainstorming ideas.

- Sell something that has value.

- Thank people for helping the volunteer group!

Don't

- Make your family do the work for the group.

- Goof off during a fund-raising event.

- Be disappointed if you don't reach your goal.

Cutout Cards

People will love buying these cards from your group!

What You'll Need

blank cards with envelopes, pencil, cookie cutters (in different shapes), craft knife and cutting mat, scrapbooking paper, scrapbooking scissors, glue, ribbon

1 Draw a shape on the front of the card with pencil. Trace around a cookie cutter or draw a shape that you like. Keep it simple!

2 Use the craft knife and the cutting mat to cut out the shape. Cut outside the pencil lines so they won't show on the card. Remember to open the card so you only cut through the top.

3 Cut a piece of scrapbooking paper. It should be big enough to cover the shape. Use scrapbooking scissors so the edges look cool!

4 Open the card and put glue around the edge of the shape. Put glue around the edges of the scrapbooking paper. Make sure you put the glue on the front side.

5 Press the scrapbooking paper over the cutout on the card. Keep the card open until the glue dries.

6 Make five more cards. Try using different shapes and paper or fabric designs. Tie the six cards and their envelopes together with a ribbon. Have everyone in your group make sets of cards. You can sell them for your next **fund-raiser**!

Out in the Community!

In school or out in the community, find ways to show your school spirit. You can wear group shirts and hats. And show a positive attitude. It will get your group noticed!

It's fun to wear your school spirit. Use the group logo or colors to make sweatshirts or totes. Wear them in school or in the community. People will know that you are part of the volunteer group. If they ask questions, tell them all about your group. It's a chance to get more students **involved** in the fun!

You can also show your spirit with your attitude. When you are volunteering, be positive. You are there to help others. Doesn't helping feel good? Show it by being friendly and following directions. Your help will be appreciated!

Support Your School!

Here are some fun ways to show your school spirit:

- Hand out group flyers.

- Wear group shirts.

- Talk with other students about your group.

- Make group posters.

- Think of ways your group can help in and out of school.

- Contact community organizations to find new volunteer opportunities.

No-Sweat Sweatshirt

It's easy to make these sweatshirts for your group!

What You'll Need

cotton sweatshirt, fabric scraps, fabric glue, fabric paint, marker, scissors

1 Lay the sweatshirt out flat. Decide what you want to show on it. Does your group help garden? Show flowers. Or maybe you read to kids. Show an open book. You can also show shapes, like hearts, stars, or a tracing of your hand.

2 Draw the shape onto the fabric with a marker. Cut out the shape. You might want to use more than one. Draw and cut out as many as you need.

3 Place the shapes on the sweatshirt. Move them around until they look just right. Then glue the shapes in place with the fabric glue.

4 Now it's time to paint. Write your group's name onto the sweatshirt.

5 Then use paint to add any extra designs. Draw lines around the shapes. Or add dots. Be creative with your new group sweatshirt!

Conclusion

What do you love about volunteering? Is it the cool people you meet? What about the interesting places you visit? Maybe you just love the feeling that you are helping. There are many things that are great about being a part of a volunteer group.

It is a way to support your school. And you meet people who like the same things as you. It's a great way to make friends and have fun. You get to achieve goals and **participate** in many different activities. This can help you become more **confident** outside of the volunteer group.

Volunteering is one cool way to show your school spirit. But it is not the only way. Check out the other books in this series. Learn about clubs and groups you can join at your school. Maybe you like dancing or cheerleading. Or maybe learning languages or playing music is your thing. There will be a club or group that fits your tastes. Take advantage of what your school has to offer. It is a great place to be!

Glossary

application – a form used to request something.

brainstorm – to come up with a solution by having all members of a group share ideas.

confident – sure of one's self and one's abilities.

culture – the behavior, beliefs, art, and other products of a particular group of people.

describe – to tell about something with words or pictures.

disaster – a sudden event that causes destruction and suffering or loss of life.

donate – to give a gift in order to help others.

donation – a gift of money or things for charity.

fund-raise – to raise money for a cause or group. A fund-raiser is an event held to raise funds.

involved – taking part in something.

participate – to take part in an activity.

perspective – a way of looking at or thinking about something.

senior – an older person.

session – a period of time used for a specific purpose or activity.

Web Sites

To learn more about cool school spirit, visit ABDO Publishing Company on the World Wide Web at **www.abdopublishing.com.** Web sites about cool school spirit are featured on our Book Links page. These links are routinely monitored and updated to provide the most current information available.

Index